Real Peo

D0858511

George W. Bush

By Mary Hill

Children's Press®
A Division of Scholastic Inc.
New York / Toronto / London / Auckland / Sydney
Mexico City / New Delhi / Hong Kong
Danbury, Connecticut

Photo Credits: Cover © Brooks Kraft/Corbis; pp. 5, 9, 15 © AFP/Corbis;
pp. 7, 13, 17, 19 © AP/Wide World Photos; p. 11 © Shelly Katz/TimePix;
p. 21 © Reuters NewMedia Inc./Corbis
Contributing Editor: Jennifer Silate
Book Design: Daniel Hosek

Library of Congress Cataloging-in-Publication Data

Hill, Mary, 1977-
    George W. Bush / by Mary Hill.
    p. cm.— (Real people)
    Includes index.
    Summary: Simple text introduces the political and family life of George
    W. Bush, who was inaugurated president of the United States in 2001.
    ISBN 0-516-25864-8 (lib. bdg.)—ISBN 0-516-27886-X (pbk.)
    1. Bush, George W. (George Walker), 1946—Juvenile literature. 2.
    Presidents—United States--Biography—Juvenile literature. 3. Bush,
    George W. (George Walker), 1946—Family--Juvenile literature. [1. Bush,
    George W. (George Walker), 1946- 2. Presidents.] I. Title. II. Series:
    Real people (Children's Press)

E903 .H55 2003
973.931'092--dc21

                                                        2002155460

Contents

Meet George W. Bush.

He is the 43rd **president** of the United States of America.

5

George was born on July 6, 1946.

He grew up in Texas with his family.

George's **wife** is
named Laura.

George and Laura have
two daughters.

George W. Bush's father was the 41st president of the United States.

His name is George Bush.

11

George W. Bush became **governor** of Texas in 1995.

He was governor for five years.

In January 2001, George W. Bush became president of the United States of America.

15

President Bush gives many **speeches**.

He tells people how he would like to make life better for Americans.

George works with other people in the **government**.

They work to make America a better place to live.

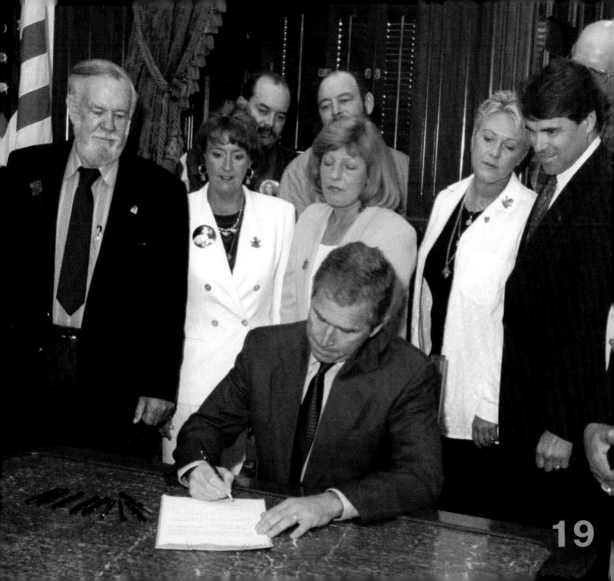

19

George W. Bush works hard for America.

21

New Words

government (**guhv**-urn-muhnt) people who rule or govern a country or state

governor (**guhv**-urn-ur) the leader of a state

president (**prez**-uh-duhnt) the leader of a country or a group of people

speeches (**speech**-uhz) talks given to groups of people

wife (**wife**) when a man and woman marry, the woman becomes the man's wife

To Find Out More

Books

George W. Bush
by Carole Marsh and Kathy Zimmer
Gallopade International

George W. Bush
by Wil Mara
Children's Press

George W. Bush: The 43rd President
by Carmen Bredeson
Enslow Publishers

Web Site

Biography of the President of the United States
http://www.whitehouse.gov/kids/president
Read about George W. Bush and find out about his
family, pets, and more on this Web site.

Index

About the Author
Mary Hill writes and edits children's books.

Reading Consultants
Kris Flynn, Coordinator, Small School District Literacy, The San Diego County Office of Education

Shelly Forys, Certified Reading Recovery Specialist, W.J. Zahnow Elementary School, Waterloo, IL

Sue McAdams, Former President of the North Texas Reading Council of the IRA, and Early Literacy Consultant, Dallas, TX